Copyright Notices

Copyright 2017 Stella Singles LLC

Disclaimer

This book and the items it distributes are for entertainment purposes only and individual results may vary. We make absolutely no guarantees, expressed or implied, that by following the advice in this guide you will achieve any results. Results will primarily depend on your personal situation, how you apply the strategies and how much experience you have. If you need professional help, please contact a therapist or a medical practitioner specializing in the field of your issue.

ISBN 9781521995082

More dating & relationship books by Stella:

What Women Really Like In A Man: 45 Dating Tips On How To
Capture A Girl's Heart, Make Her Fall In Love With You (For Good)
and Never Want To Leave You

Read Her Signs: An Essential Guide To Understanding Women and
Never Getting Rejected Again

The Road To Confidence: Learn to Conquer Your Fears, Build Self-
Confidence and Enjoy Long-Lasting Dating Success

FLIRT HER *UP*

HOW TO USE THE POWER OF WORDS AND BODY LANGUAGE TO ATTRACT, INTERACT AND CONNECT WITH WOMEN IN ANY SETTING

By Stella Belmar

http://www.StellaDatingCoach.com

http://www.StellaSingles.com

ISBN 9781521995082

Table of Contents

INTRODUCTION 1

APPEARANCE 8

ATTITUDE..15

CORE PRINCIPLES OF FLIRTING....................19

TWO KEY INGREDIENTS 20

Your Mindset 23

Your Posture 24

    Entering the room 24

    Moving toward the girl target.........................26

YOUR ATTITUDE AND BEHAVIOR 35

WHO YOU ARE 44

FLIRTING...46

DETACHMENT 46

TALKING 47

    External Focus..47

    Silence is golden...49

    Let's talk about… 50

CONVERSATION TACTICS 56

    Making Statements..57

    Creating and using hooks 60

    Giving Compliments 62

    Sexual Innuendo 65

Exaggeration 67

Role Playing 68

Us Against Them...71

TOUCH.. 72

CHEMISTRY 73

BALANCING ACT 76

ENERGY 82

SPREAD THE WORD 83

Your Free Bonus

Thank you for purchasing this book. I hope it will be a helpful tool on your journey to being successful with women.

To further help you along, I've included 2 free bonuses that you won't want to miss. One discusses **tests that women put men through and why it's important not to fail at these.** And the second one talks about **how to move the interaction from flirting to sex**. Enjoy!

Type the URL below to receive your gift:

http://www.subscribepage.com/womentests

FLIRT HER *UP*

HOW TO USE THE POWER OF WORDS AND BODY LANGUAGE TO ATTRACT, INTERACT AND CONNECT WITH WOMEN IN ANY SETTING

By Stella Belmar

INTRODUCTION

Flirting. Charm. Seduction. These are all words that get thrown around a lot, yet few people really master their true meaning and even fewer know how to make them work for them.

Yet, in the world of dating and relationships, attraction, personal interaction, smooth conversation and a sleek approach can often make all the difference.

In this book, I will show you the secrets of **flirting** and how to use those skills and techniques appropriately to get the desired results. European men have mastered these techniques thanks to a more liberal upbringing and a natural way of relating to women.

Players and women seducers in the U.S. also master some flirting techniques, but they use it in a manipulative way most of the time, completely missing out on the real advantages and additional possibilities that a more sophisticated form of flirting can bring.

If you're a nice man, but find it difficult to leave your shell or talk to women in a charming way, read on. If you're a geek who's very smart, but maybe somewhat awkward with approaching a girl, read on. If you're a regular guy that wants to polish his flirting skills to be more attractive to women and get the girls he desires, read on.

This guide will expand your horizons no matter what kind of man you really are. The fact alone that you're reading this book is proof that you're on the right path to success. Navigating the world of dating and relationships can be challenging. We don't go to school for this. We learn by trial, error, and by studying the behavior of others, whether it be various techniques that men apply, or advice from women on what works on them. Mastering those skills can bring you light years ahead of the competition and help you succeed in your main goal: bringing the right woman to you. Bottom line, even if you've retained one useful item after reading this book, my job has been done.

I wish you much success as you master the skill of flirting, and look forward to giving you opportunities you otherwise would have missed out on!

THE BASICS

If you Google the word 'flirt', the first definition that pops up is most likely: "to behave as though sexually attracted to someone, but playfully rather than with serious intentions."

Wikipedia further states that flirting "usually involves speaking and behaving in a way that suggests a mildly greater intimacy than the actual relationship between the parties would justify, though within the rules of social etiquette, which generally disapproves of a direct expression of sexual interest in the given setting." It explains that flirting can be done by communicating a sense of playfulness or irony.

If you read those definitions carefully, you'll notice that they both refer to "playfulness," "irony," and "as though sexually attracted." This is the point I'd like to drive home with this book: The biggest mistake men make is that they take flirting too fast and too far (sexually). They use flirting techniques too aggressively and take the whole thing too seriously.

And by doing so, they lose on the subtleties and sophistication that come with the real mastery of this 'art.' You end up missing out on much more than you may have even dreamed of with the girl you never thought you could catch.

Flirting is an art, but also a skill anyone can learn. Some are better at it than others. Some have practiced more and thus know quite well how to apply their skills to any setting. Others have made a point of learning this 'skill' and perfecting it to an 'art' of their own.

Whatever the way, learning and practicing flirting can only be beneficial to you. It not only allows you to feel and behave confidently around women, but it also allows you to get out of your head, open up and notice that women are impatient for you to make your move!

So, let's dig in.

THE GOAL

Before we jump into the various techniques, you need to understand the purpose or goal of flirting.

What it is:

- Flirting should be used to approach women seamlessly, to get noticed by women and to spark their interest.
- Flirting is a tool to have a casual conversation with a woman you're interested in.
- Flirting can contain very subtle sexual undertones.
- Flirting happens with the goal of creating attraction and chemistry with women.
- Flirting shows that you're a man who is confident in his own skin and who masters the art of talking and displaying his charm with women.
- Flirting will quickly make you stand out from your competition so that the most attractive woman of the group will notice your presence, which in turn will improve your chances of being with her.
- Flirting is a way of life and can be practiced with random strangers as an exchange of mutual appreciation between parties.
- Flirting needs to become part of who you are, while you still need to maintain control as to when and how you use this skill.

- Flirting is a behavior and attitude that can be learned and practiced.
- Flirting techniques are non-exhaustive: this means that there are always additional ways you can come up with to flirt and charm women.
- Flirting is personal: a man's flirting style needs to be in harmony with his personality and become an integral part of who he is.
- Flirting includes more than just words. It's a holistic system using words, actions, gestures and non-verbal language to maximize the message that a woman receives from you.
- Anyone can master flirting. Whether you're ugly, old, short, poor, geeky, awkward or shy, be reassured that you too can learn how to flirt and attract women seamlessly.
- Flirting should always result in a win-win situation.

What it is NOT:

- Flirting should not contain overly sexual statements or aggressive invitations for sexual acts.
- Flirting is NOT directly used to get a woman in bed that same night (even though in some instances it may happen, direct sex is NOT the goal of flirting.)
- Flirting should never contain vulgarity, force, disrespect or harassment of a woman.
- Flirting is not a tool to manipulate women or use it for other dishonest purposes.

- Flirting should not happen in an environment that does not call for it, such as overtly flirting at work and other professional places, with married women, etc.
- Flirting is not a game where one person wins and the other loses.
- Flirting does not guarantee that the person you're flirting with will absolutely want to date you, have sex with you or be in a relationship with you.
- Flirting is not a talent that some people have and others don't. Rather, it's a skill that anyone can learn and practice.

Please re-read those two lists and make sure you understand every bullet point. In this guide, we'll be going into a more detailed analysis of what flirting entails, but the above list is paramount in understanding the overall premise of this advice.

BEFORE YOU START

As I already mentioned, flirting needs to be or become a key part of a man's personality. As a matter of fact, many women will make a distinction between a boy and a man by the way you flirt, or even by whether you flirt or not and how comfortable you feel doing it. Trust me, you want to land in the man category.

It doesn't matter what age you are, what you do for a living or how you look. Flirting can transform your personality to the point that women will flock to you.

But before we dig deeper into it, let's review what makes a man attractive to a woman and the basics you need to have in place BEFORE you even try to flirt.

APPEARANCE

You don't need to be a model: good looking, slim and tall. But you do need to keep a clean appearance if you want women to find you attractive.

And by clean, I mean not just fresh as in just out of the shower. That's of course the first requirement. But the overall appearance also includes the way you dress, the type of clothes you wear, whether you shave and how your hair looks.

There are many frogs out there that women have to sift through, let alone kiss, before finding one that is attractive enough to even bother talking with. A woman can be quickly disgusted if a guy is dirty looking, and this includes everything from smelling bad, having dirty teeth or ears, wearing wrinkled or dirty clothes, baggy and sagging pants, worn-out shoes, etc.

That's why, as a first rule, you need to pay extra careful attention to your physical appearance.

Here are some pointers:

- Take a shower before you go out and never allow yourself to smell bad, whether it's sweat, or the smell of fried oil coming off your clothes as if you just walked out of a McDonald's.
- I know it's fashionable to have a goatee or something similar, but as a rule of thumb, most women still prefer a clean-shaven guy. If you take good care of yours and look trendy, more power to you. But if it's not well taken care of, you'd better shave it off and have a clean, smooth face.
- Greasy hair or hair that is too long and doesn't have a nice shape is definitely a turn-off. Again, you don't need to have the hair of a model, but get a regular hair cut so that it looks neat.

- Nails that are too long or dirty is a huge no-no. Dirt is absolutely unacceptable under nails, whether it's on the fingers or on your toes. Some guys think, for whatever reason, that having grown-out (I am not even mentioning long) nails is ok. For most women, it is NOT ok. And let me tell you why. A man with long nails can hurt a woman if he's touching her in her intimate parts. So, a man who keeps his nails long, meaning that he doesn't cut them short to the skin, is a sure giveaway that he's either not gentle with a woman when they are intimate, has no intimacy skills or experience with women, has not gotten laid in a long time or is in general clueless about what it takes to be with a woman. Also, nails that are even slightly long will give you a feminine vibe, which is very unattractive to women. Appealing men keep their nails short and clean! I hope this was enough to convince you to ALWAYS keep your nails in good order.
- Trim that nose and/or ear hair.
- Ok, so you may have a belly. Don't shut yourself out just because of this or any other imperfection. Instead, find a way to camouflage it by wearing an appropriate shirt that enhances your overall elegance so that the attention is directed to other parts of your body or clothing. For example, if you're wearing a sparkling clean shirt that just came out of the dry cleaners, it will enhance your overall appearance, even if you have a belly. On the other hand, if you wear baggy shorts and an old sports T-shirt that highlights your 'curve,' that's clearly a bad move. Men who attract women are those who know how to dress for the occasion and it's usually a

smart idea to overdress rather than underdress. Don't be too casual, instead make it a point to look nice and you'll be already ahead of your competition.

- Make sure to take good care of your skin, especially on the face. If you happen to have pimples or other imperfections, take appropriate care of those and minimize the after-effects. Don't leave blackheads, whiteheads or other skin lesions sit there as if it's ok. You'd find it gross on a woman, so that's also valid for you. Apply creams to your face, hands and feet regularly if they tend to run dry. You don't need to become like a woman, but take care of your body. These days, many men will use hydrating creams for the face, and body lotions for dry patches of skin.

- Wear perfume or cologne! In Europe, many men and women will spray perfume on every morning before they get out of the house. They'll do another round at night if they go out. It's a great habit to have and gives you a hint of sophistication. Separate yourself from the crowd and wear some nice cologne. This too will attract women. Why do you think those scents exist in the first place?

- Another reason for wearing cologne is that smell is important to attract a mate. Studies prove that women are attracted to a man via his smell. And every man smells differently. Some men smell so good naturally that women just can't resist them. They most likely have a strong dose of endorphins that they release with their natural smell. And we all know that these are nature's way of attracting the opposite sex. Now, you need to understand that only one in 10 or even 30 men may have

11

the right smell for the woman he meets. So, it's best to assume that you don't have this kind of high-endorphin-releasing natural smell. That's why it's 'safer' to wear a cologne or perfume that will slightly camouflage your natural smell and instead send a hint of freshness and a nice aroma to women, spiking their interest before they can potentially get turned off by your natural smell. It's not a statement about you or that you stink. Not at all. It's just the way nature has created men and women. There's not much either one can do about it, but you can certainly enhance your sex appeal by other means.

- In regards to chains, bracelets, piercings, etc., wear those ONLY if this is THE statement you want to make about yourself, meaning if it's truly a part of your identity and you want to attract a woman that may appreciate it. Otherwise, please refrain from wearing golden chains, chains with crosses, bracelets or even rings. A man with a golden chain around his neck gives the impression of being part of the Italian mafia, or being flashy or cocky. It's really not attractive to women. Bracelets and rings are not as bad, but they too send a signal of weirdness or unusualness about you. It's always best to appear as normal as possible. Key is not to direct attention of a potential conquest to unnecessary elements in your appearance. You want everything to play to your advantage. Energy and attention from the woman you desire needs to flow to your face, what you say and your non-verbal communication. You don't want her to get stuck on an element in your appearance that would stray her away from the real message and real flirting you will be doing. A silver chain with a cross sends a strong signal that you may be excessively religious, or that you're a mama's boy and are wearing it because you feel it pleases her. Whatever the underlying reason, a man's man keeps his appearance traditional, yet elegant. And this means no jewelry.

- Fresh breath: it's hard to assess yourself whether your breath smells. But to be sure that it doesn't, brush your teeth and/or rinse it with Listerine or a similar product. You can also carry chewing gum or mints with you and use those right before going to a party, a bar, a date or any other gathering. There's nothing more gross than a man whose breath smells bad. It could be from personal hygiene or from stomach problems or from the foods you eat, but it's a huge turn off. How do you think a woman would imagine kissing you if your breath smells bad? That's a surefire way to send any woman running, so pay attention to it.

- Don't wear those sandals! I repeat: Don't wear those sandals. I have said it before and I am saying it again: unless you have model-looking feet, exposing your manly toes and naked feet in those heavy rubber sandals is a big no-no if you want to look attractive to women. Even if you're living in a hot climate and are meeting someone during the day, wear closed shoes. You'd be better off wearing sport shoes or any other kind of closed shoe than sandals. Believe me, most girls really don't like staring at a guy's big feet. So, hide them. You can always wear them later, when the two of you already know each other.

- I would also like to point out that shoes say a big deal about a man. If you're wearing cheap, worn-out or dirty shoes, it immediately sends a message that you're either poor, lack sophistication or are not so clean. Even if the rest of your clothing is not expensive, invest some money in nice shoes and wear them when you're planning to date or flirt with women. It will immediately give you a competitive advantage over other guys that don't pay attention to this element.

- Dress for the occasion. If you're going to a happening place that's outdoors and a band is playing at night, don't show up in shorts, sandals and some baggy T-shirt, even if it's hot outside. Also, don't show up in a suit as if it's a business meeting. Instead, dress the part. You can wear jeans with a nice belt and a clean shirt. Put on socks and nice shoes. Be a little trendy – even if you're a conservative guy. Wear cologne. You'll make yourself much more attractive than that sloppy guy next to you hanging over his beer. Same goes for other events. It's always better to be slightly overdressed than underdressed.

ATTITUDE

A lot of your success with women will depend on your attitude. It's an all-encompassing term and we'll be referring to it throughout this book and the tips I will be sharing with you.

But let's start with some general guidelines about how your overall attitude and the way you carry yourself influences everything from whom you attract, to how the world perceives you, to your ultimate success with getting the woman you want.

Everyone always says that women like confident men. But what does it really mean? Confidence is something easier said than done for many people.

If you're feeling down and have a low opinion of yourself, you're not the only one. As a matter of fact, I think most people struggle with self-confidence issues at least a few times during their lives. It is something you need to always work on, but there are some shortcuts that you can take to speed up the process and to help you in your journey with women. As one will say: "Fake it 'til you make it." This is especially true when it comes to appearing self-confident.

Here are some tips to get you started:

- A confident man doesn't hesitate, doesn't change his mind all the time and doesn't vacillate among various choices.
- That said, he also knows when to be flexible and when to stand his ground. Unreasonableness either way is never good. Be balanced and adjust your course when necessary.

- He takes the leadership role, but he doesn't impose himself.

- He's not needy or desperate. Instead, he knows his value and respects himself, but also others.

- He's not controlling. Leadership doesn't mean you're trying to control the other person. It's a very important distinction to make. Many men confuse the two. You will look attractive to a woman when you're leading her and deciding where to take her on a date or what to do. You will start losing your appeal if you start to control the woman herself: what she does, how she does it, what she wears, what she eats etc. It may seem like a fine line, but you need to become a master in distinguishing the two.

- He's independent and knows where he's going in life. Women like men who know what they want. Again, there is a difference between knowing what you want and imposing a selfish agenda. The first is about you, the second is about the relationship and not taking into consideration the other person. In my book, *What Women Really Like in a Man*, I describe this and other elements in more detail.

- A confident man also doesn't put others down, isn't arrogant or self-serving. He's a gentleman and a giver, because he knows that giving puts him in a position of being a strong person.

- Smile and be social. It's the guys who smile and are confident in their body who attract the most attention. If you're hiding in a corner or behind a glass of beer, you immediately send a message of awkwardness or unease to a woman – and that's not very attractive.

- Hold yourself straight. Don't justify yourself regarding any mishaps you may have done and don't raise your voice for any reason. This doesn't mean you can't apologize when you've done wrong. But don't unnecessarily put yourself in a guilty spot before the verdict is out.

- A confident guy also doesn't talk like crazy or over others. He can just as easily stand and listen in a very interesting pose and be attractive to a woman. As a matter of fact, that's one way of creating mystery, and women like that. So, even if you're nervous or stressed, try to control the chatting and pay more attention to what she's saying. A guy who can't stop talking is not only a turnoff, but he also appears self-centered, unstable, nervous or womanlike. Train yourself to listen more to others. It's a win-win not just in relationships but also in life.

- Don't make funny faces if you're disgusted by something or don't like something. It's understandable that not everyone likes the same kinds of foods, for example. But if you start making a gross face because you're smelling fish at the table next to you at a restaurant, it's a huge turn off to the girl. It shows that you're not tolerant, that you may be picky, that you may be a clean freak, or worse, that you'll be grossed out by certain intimate things. It's a kiss of death to do this, so don't.

- Don't criticize everyone and everything. Try to maintain a positive attitude. If you can't say something nice, then don't say it. You want to appear as positive as possible, but make sure not to fake it either. If you're overdoing it, then it will be obvious. So, find a way to create a balanced attitude for yourself that evaluates the world and others in a mild and objective way.

- Write down some of the core values that are important to you. Once you've zeroed in on those, use them proudly in conversations and actions. A woman likes a man with strong values, so stick to them and display them. This will bring you immediate respect.

- Don't show off how much you make or what kind of job you have. The best way is to mention it casually, but if you're making good money and think you may attract a woman this way, overdoing it will backfire. It's good to be proud about it, but don't put it as number 1 of your conversation. If you're doing well, it will become obvious quickly. And if you're not doing so well, no need to go into too much detail too soon.

- A confident man doesn't put women down or insult them; he isn't bitter that women are 'gold diggers' or 'users'; he also doesn't use vulgarity in describing his 'hunt' for women. Ban these words from your vocabulary. If you believe in these stereotypes, then you're not ready to be an appealing man who is in charge of his destiny and in control of his life. Guys who are successful with women love women – they don't hate them. If you have issues from a prior divorce or bad dating experiences, you need to work through those first before trying to get women. As long as you are prisoner to negative and self-destructive beliefs, everything will fail in your life, and you may not even realize it until it's too late. So, before blaming women or others for your failures, look deep inside and see how you can become a better person. You are the result of everything you've thought of, said and done in your life. You and only you are responsible for where you're at now. So, don't blame others. Instead, take responsibility to become a better you – SO THAT YOU CAN ATTRACT THE WOMAN YOU WANT!

CORE PRINCIPLES
OF FLIRTING

Men in the field can be broadly categorized into two major extremes: the players, who have mastered the art of flirting and attracting women, but often use it in a self-serving or manipulative way; and those we'll call the good guys, who have good intentions but lack experience in the flirting arena.

Your goal is to land in the in-between category: you want to be a good guy with good intentions who knows how to engage a woman, how to make her feel comfortable with you and how to create a good rapport with her so that she would be interested in pursuing something more with you. Many men in relationships, whether it's with a girlfriend or a wife, fall into this category. Even if your direct goal is not to be in a relationship, eventually this may be the case in your life, so it's best to be ready for this anyways. Also, the skills required for casual or serious dating are pretty much the same.

These normal guys have either learned from their mistakes and used their experience to succeed in the dating game, or have had the chance of learning from role models such as fathers or friends who exemplified the right behaviors with women.

Either way, what's important is that this is a skill that anybody can learn. Many men who are successful have probably read at least one dating self-help book and thoroughly studied what works and what doesn't work with women.

This is also the main reason why guys in relationships are usually more attractive to single women. They seem to know how to relate to women, and they take the necessary actions to take care of their girl and make them feel loved and appreciated. It is not so much the approval of another woman that makes them so appealing to others. The key element is that they are more relaxed, not needy or desperate, don't play games, don't try to manipulate or put down women. Instead, they respect women and treat them nicely, no matter what. They have mastered the most important character traits that make them desirable. And you can too!

TWO KEY INGREDIENTS

If you want to be successful in flirting and attracting women, two key personality traits play a role. It's always good to keep these in mind and to try to improve in both areas.

1. Self-Worth

Call it self-esteem, self-value, self-confidence or self-worth, the most important thing to remember is that it relates to how you perceive yourself. It's something that is generated internally and resides in your subconscious self. Others also perceive it rather subconsciously about you.

That said, you can always improve in this area if you don't feel good about yourself. There are plenty of books that discuss how to improve your self-esteem and how to value yourself better.

It is VERY IMPORTANT to keep working on this aspect of yourself if you want to succeed in the dating and flirting game. By the way, I am using the word 'game' as a metaphor for the dating arena and not literally as in that you need to play games.

Anyway, if you don't feel good about yourself, how can you feel confident and comfortable approaching women? Remember that women have a very fine-tuned intuition and are very perceptive. They will quickly sense how much value you assign yourself.

That's not to say you need to be cocky or arrogant. These are external behaviors and usually indicate that you have low self-worth and thus are trying to compensate for it.

In this book, we'll go into more detail about what self-worth or self-value means when flirting with women and what they perceive as a high-value man. There are certainly ways you can improve to send a signal of high value to women.

2. Your Attitude/Behavior

The second key ingredient is your general attitude, which translates into your behavior or actions toward women. This is just as important as your self-worth as it can compensate in some areas you may be lacking and vice versa.

Remember, no one is perfect and we're not trying to make you a machine that perfectly executes a code. You always need to use common sense and pick things that fit with your personality and who you are.

As a matter of fact, it is paramount to cultivate your own unique way of being with and talking to women. At the end of the day, that's what will make them really like you, not some silly pick-up line you read in a book and practiced at home before going out.

There are many behaviors you can learn and practice to get good at attracting women. These behaviors are easy to learn, but practice makes perfect. No matter how awkward or inexperienced you are, you can learn it just like any other skill.

When you look at how much time and effort you put into learning job-specific skills or educate yourself in life, it only makes sense to study up a bit on flirting techniques in order to get better at the other 50% of what your life is all about: attracting women, dating and relationships.

YOUR VALUE OR SELF-WORTH

The kind of self-worth you assign yourself translates into two parts: the value you give yourself, and that subtle energy that shines through you to others. Self-worth resides mostly in your subconscious and women usually pick up on this from your non-verbal communication.

We've all heard that over 60% of how humans communicate happens in the non-verbal form. This is especially true in flirting. And the way you feel about yourself will directly translate into your body language and other ways of being.

While the deeper psychological issues of low self-esteem are not the direct scope of this book, what you can do in the context of flirting with and attracting women is to work on the external signs that will communicate to women subconsciously how you value yourself. It's a tricky territory in a sense that it's not that easy to hide the vibe you send to others. But you can help it along with the below techniques.

YOUR MINDSET

The key to any dating, flirting or seduction is to have the right mindset. If you feel anger, frustration, desperation or laziness about approaching and dating women, you will subconsciously sabotage yourself. Even if you try all the techniques in this book but you keep a negative mindset, people will perceive this and will quickly turn their attention to someone else.

So before you engage in any kind of pick-up or flirting behavior, ask yourself: "Am I doing this for the right reasons? Do I actually want to be with this girl Do I actually like women or am I trying to be a manipulative jerk? Do I feel that I deserve to be with the right woman or do I not value myself?"

If you notice a hint of any kind of negative emotion, feeling or intention, I urge you to take notice and consciously decide to correct that internal state, or at the very least be more aware of it. By bringing emotions to the surface of our awareness, we can almost always change anything in ourselves we don't appreciate. So, look yourself (figuratively) in the mirror and see what elements you don't like and toss them out. It doesn't need to be complicated. You have the power. You just need to decide to do so!

YOUR POSTURE

Entering the room

Whether you're tall or short, slim or chubby, there is a way of carrying yourself that will immediately call a woman's attention. It's the way you hold yourself and the way you walk.

Stand straight, with your head and face looking forward, not down. When you walk into a room or a public place, keep this straight stature. Walk with a purpose. Claim your physical space around you.

Be careful not to behave like you're a total 'star' and send a 'macho' message to the room. But having a prouder posture can go a long way. Look further out and focus on something specific in that place, whether it's the bar area, a restaurant table, a box office or the cashier's counter in a store. When you stand and walk with purpose, it immediately creates an air of a man who knows what he wants and where he's going. And that's very sexy to women.

When you're meeting a woman and she's already there, for example sitting at a table in a restaurant, don't immediately search for her when you first walk into the place. Instead, first things first: talk to the host or waiter about where to sit or ask where she may be sitting. If it's a coffee shop and there is no host to talk to, then walk in, stand still for a second or two until it's clear you have assessed the place and are comfortable with the surroundings. Then turn your head to see where the girl may be sitting.

If you're at a party or a public gathering, keep your purposeful stature and way of moving around the room. Don't just jump on any girl that looks attractive and hit her up. Take a moment to evaluate the environment, then make yourself comfortable and only then make moves towards a woman or women you may be interested in.

If you're slouching forward, holding your beer in front of you as if to protect you from a big bear, hesitant or bouncing from one side to the other of the room, you'll send an immediate signal of a man who's insecure, wishy-washy and unsure of himself. That's a big turnoff to women.

Moving toward the girl target

1. WHEN YOU'RE MEETING SOMEONE SPECIFIC, SUCH AS A BLIND DATE, AN ONLINE DATE OR ANY OTHER FIRST DATE

When you do start moving toward the woman you're meeting, it's time to become more relaxed. This is when your facial expressions will become more important. A man who sends a signal of being interesting and knowing where he's going will slightly change his posture. It will shift from a very straight, almost formal posture, to a warmer and more relaxed body movement toward the woman. You don't need to stand as straight as before but can slightly relax yourself and open up your body in the direction you're going. Pull your arms slightly out to your sides so that they don't hang down so straight. It's almost like you're preparing to give someone a hug, only this time you may not do it (depending on your situation of course).

Keep in mind this needs to be a subtle shift, not a full-blown movement. The point is to have slightly different body language than when you just walked in. Create a slight cup-like body position with your chest just a tad more retreated to the back than your arms, a more rounded posture. Again, this needs to be just very slight, to make you appear warmer and less serious or stiff.

Continue walking with purpose, though, until you're sitting or standing by the woman. . The key is to have this shift in posture. A man with many sides to his personality and who is charming and appealing to women adjusts his body depending on the setting and situation. If you're always staying the same, it can send a signal that you're boring, nervous or stiff. The key is to always be aware of how you carry yourself. Awareness is attractive, whether in men or women. And this is just the start.

2. WHEN YOU'RE IN A PUBLIC SETTING WITH VARIOUS POTENTIAL GIRLS YOU'D LIKE TO MEET THAT YOU DON'T KNOW YET

The situation is different when you're at a party or another public event where there are women you'd like to meet, but you don't know any of them yet.

It is still important to move around the room in a purposeful way, holding your body straight, but not stiff or formal. You need to be relaxed but stand tall and claim the physical space around you.

When you want to strike a conversation with a woman, first keep your body slightly sideways. Do not come at her straight as this may create an element of unease and may invade her space unnecessarily. Also, it's too direct and too focused on her, which sends her a signal that you're on the hunt.

It's safer and more prudent to come closer to a girl with the side of your body. In the animal kingdom, dogs for example, this is considered a friendly, non-threatening approach. Approaching another dog straight on is an aggressive move and is intimidating. You don't want to be that way with the woman you're about to connect with.

When you start developing a conversation, then it's ok to turn toward her completely. But still, don't come too close where you invade her boundaries. It's very unpleasant for women to have a guy who's hanging all over them. Keep a polite distance and build on it only as time passes and you're sensing rapport building.

.

FACIAL EXPRESSION

When men are out and about, they tend to have a more serious facial expression than women, in general. And that's ok, as you can give off an air of mystery and internal charisma.

However, it's also important for a man to soften his traits once he's initiated contact with a woman. By contact, I mean it could be eye contact, seeing your planned date from afar or striking up a fresh conversation with a stranger. What makes a man magnetic is the change in facial expression. Don't always keep a serious face. And don't run around with a smile and a look like you're ready to hit on the first chick you meet. Again, just as with your body posture, the importance lies in being more expressive than your average guy.

Your facial expression needs to agree with the now. Depending on the situation and the person you're approaching, you need to make adjustments, as naturally as possible, that would reflect your internal state and your intention. A man who is sure of himself and his value will have an expression that's coherent with the moment. It sends an air of confidence, a key attractor.

A facial expression can tell a lot about you and your intentions, so be aware of the message you're sending. However, the most important thing is to send a message of friendliness before anything else. That's the basis of any human connection.

But that's also just the starting point.

1. WHEN YOU KNOW HER

Just as you like when your girl's face lights up when she sees you, a woman will appreciate it when your face lights up when you suddenly see her sitting at the table, you find her among a group of people or pick her up at home. Smile and show her you're happy to see her. Be expressive. This raises your vibrancy and creates an aura of positive energy between the two of you.

2. WHEN YOU DON'T KNOW HER

If you're approaching a woman for the first time, change your facial expression to a smile when you start talking with her, not when you're walking toward her. There is a difference between smiling and sending a wink to a girl from afar and smiling too much as you're walking toward her. Do the smiling specifically for her. This will make her feel special. Women like knowing you picked them over someone else. So, keep your tender moves reserved for when you interact with her.

3. FLIRTING EXPRESSIONS

Now let's get into the nitty-gritty. A lot can be said just by the way you look at someone and your facial expression.

For instance, there are diverse types of smiles you can have. Sending a more flirtatious or sensuous smile is different from smiling at her because you really like her. One is more seductive, the other is friendlier. One sends a slightly sexual signal, the other sends a signal of appreciation.

Observe yourself. Observe guys you know who are good with women. See how their faces change depending on the girl, the situation and their intent. Cultivate and practice different smiles. But always remember, don't overdo it and don't try to be someone you're not. If it looks rehearsed, you'll chase the girl away even faster than you can say hello. Some guys sometimes produce a smirk and that looks not just bad, but also artificial. It emits a signal of discomfort with yourself and with your girl.

Instead, practice to always be relaxed and detached from the outcome. That's why the first smile should just be a neutral friendly smile. You need to increase your body language and expressions step by step so as not to come on too strong. Be too direct or too pushy, and she's gone. Start gently and slowly and move from there. This will create a safe environment for you and for her. Once you see she's starting to relax, you can turn it up a bit. But keep with what's going on in the moment – don't just keep smiling non-stop. Change up your expression depending on what is said, how she's reacting, etc.

If you make a witty comment or a joke, you can look at her with a perplexed face to see if she understood. You can give her a quick wink, but use this one very sparingly and only much later into your conversation. Maximum one wink per evening and even that can be too much. You need to feel it before doing it!

When you smile, don't smile with your full mouth open. This gives away too much of your energy and looks more like a friendly, happy smile, instead of a seductive one. Don't show too much teeth either. Instead, smile lightly and pair that with some significant eye contact. This is much more attractive to a woman.

4. EYE CONTACT

This is one of the most important parts of flirting. Eyes convey so much to a person. Women will not only pick up on your intentions, but they'll also read you and what you're about by looking into your eyes. This latter part is something you cannot control, so don't even try to hide whatever you want to hide. The best strategy is to be relaxed and natural.

A quick note on women's intuition and how they read what kind of a man you are. As we know, women are highly intuitive. They will see through you in no time, but there's not much you can do about this. That's why you need to always strive to be the best person you can in everything you do. No one is perfect, but the key is to always work on yourself. The more positive you become, the more of that vibe women will get just by looking at you and into your eyes.

A woman can quickly read through your eyes whether you're honest or a liar, whether you're a straight shooter or a game player, whether you're a smart guy or not so much, whether you're gentle or if you can be ice cold. Keep those in mind and cultivate a culture of pleasantness everywhere you go. It will translate into your facial expression and into your eyes. Don't forget this! Eyes are your major asset when flirting with women.

For example, one of the worst things to have are shifty eyes. Sometimes it can happen to a shy person. Also, someone who's not feeling comfortable or who is dishonest can have shifty eyes. It's hard to know whether that's the case with you or not, but if anyone ever told you this, it may be that that's the case. Best thing is to ask your parents, siblings or friends about how they would describe your eyes. To avoid having shifty eyes, practice focusing on your target, whether it's an object you're looking at, a person, a door, a book, anything. When you look with purpose and focus, you'll avoid the risk of having a shifty look. On the other hand, if you're drunk, on drugs, or trying to hide something, your eyes may get shifty.

Another mistake people make is having a blank stare. You will quickly send a signal of a man who may be boring, dumb, not interesting, indifferent or not interested in the woman. When you're with her, look at her. See if you can smile with your eyes. Practice 'talking' with your eyes. You can say so much without saying a word.

There is a song that goes: "We made love with nothing but our eyes." This is your goal. See if you can send a signal of warmth, compassion, understanding, respect and even attraction with your eyes. Books have been written on just this subject. If you'd like to know more, feel free to dig into this topic. The worst thing is not to be expressive.

Now you may say: "This is all good and well, but what if I'm feeling super nervous about this girl?" Well, the secret not to feel so nervous is to view every encounter as a potential friendship and not someone you need to absolutely score with. Be detached from the outcome. Don't take anything personally, even if you're being rejected. More often than not, women may not pay attention to you not because of anything you say or do, but for a reason that has nothing to do with you.

This is why I keep repeating that you need to cultivate a sense of detachment within yourself. If it's not working with this one, then it will work with another one. If you're sensing that she's not feeling it, then maybe it's not meant to be. And if there is no chemistry, there is nothing either one of you can do to change that. You either click with someone or you don't – it's that simple. The most important thing to remember is that you will click with someone else sooner or later. All you can do is try to improve in areas you're lacking and be your best self at every step of the way.

Conveying humor with your eyes is also easy. You've probably heard of smiling with your eyes. Do this and cultivate a warmth that shines through you.

Some men have very deep eyes. For example, a woman will look into those deep brown eyes and just melt. You can improve on that by slightly making your eyes smaller and by looking in a focused way at the woman, as if you're trying to read inside her. But be careful not to do it in an invasive way. Instead, just keep your stare one second longer so as to really look deeply into her eyes. Then turn away and say something or do something.

Another example is the purity of a blue-eyed look. If you're thinking about something more touchy or sensitive while looking at the girl, you may send an amazing signal that is just so mesmerizing.

Of course, not everyone can do that or has those eyes. Don't worry. You just need to put your strongest features forward and practice a little about things you didn't pay attention to in the past.

Big no-no's in eye contact is to look at a woman as if you're going to undress her. This makes women immediately very uncomfortable and transgresses their boundaries. Staring is never good. If you're sending an uninterested or indifferent look, for example when a woman joins your immediate circle at a conference, it is not going to attract anyone. If you're so busy talking with your buddies about whatever it is and not noticing that a woman has just joined the group, you're not only unattractive to her but also to others who may be observing you at a distance. If you want to have a magnetic personality, then you need to always acknowledge a woman's presence and be nice to her.

Finally, some men, especially business men, can have cold eyes. Ok, you're a business man and you're serious about what you do. I get that. But if you're like that in business, you needn't be like this in private. And to avoid it, be more expressive everywhere, even at work. The more you cultivate a strong energy that flows through you, the more charismatic you will become.

YOUR ATTITUDE AND BEHAVIOR

You can't have congruent and powerful behavior if you have a bad attitude. Men who are successful with women will openly say that they like, love and respect women. They will not bash them, blame them or put them down. It's that simple.

There are many things that may be blocking you from realizing your full potential with women. You may believe you are not worthy, that all women are bad, that you're unlucky in love, that you're ugly, fat or poor. These negative thoughts will all sabotage your success with women. It may be good to make a checklist of things that bother you in women and/or your private life. Be honest with yourself and see how you can work through those issues. If necessary, see a therapist. The less baggage you have the better off you'll be in your pursuit of meeting and dating women.

Many men get stuck on those issues. Women are used to talking things out and moving on despite obstacles. Guy tend to linger on harm that has been done to them, without realizing that's exactly what is holding them back. Become aware of your issues and try to close any unfinished business. You'll be doing yourself and that cute girl a huge favor.

If you have a good attitude, it will translate into positive and constructive behaviors with women. And there are many actions and behaviors you can take. The practical actions of a gentleman that will make you stand out as charming and different from others are mostly outlined in my book, "*What Women Really Like in a Man*.

Here, we'll go directly into more specific flirting behaviors. These are the easiest to learn and to practice. All you need to do is go out to places and events where you can meet women and just practice, without setting any goals for yourself with that woman. Just relax, be natural and try your behaviors on various women. If something is flopping, no big deal, just move on.

But before we go any further, let's focus on one of the most important determinants of success with women. Why do women prefer some men and not others? Why do women get attracted to jerks and men who don't treat them right? Why do nice or good guys have it so hard with women?

The one-word answer to this is: ATTRACTION.

And how do you build attraction? By being MASCULINE.

It's that simple. And it's that complicated. Why? Because bad boys display masculine behaviors, while the nice guys gravitate toward more feminine behaviors.

Once you understand this, it will be key to attracting women and being successful with them.

So how does a masculine man act?

- He's not afraid of women.
- He doesn't put women on a pedestal.
- He doesn't care too much what others think of him or whether they'll judge him for his actions.
- He's true to himself. He's authentic to his values. These are usually strong values of integrity, honesty and leadership.
- He's a gentleman, but knows what he wants.
- He exudes confidence.
- He's secure in himself.
- He's driven and ambitious.
- He knows he can tackle any challenge that comes his way.
- He doesn't complain, exhibit excessive emotional ups and downs and behaves in a difficult manner.
- He embodies all of the elements of a good attitude toward women.
- He doesn't immediately attach himself emotionally to women. Instead, he first builds a rapport and a connection to see where it can go and whether he's compatible with a woman.
- If he's being rejected, he moves on without bitterness or angriness.

- He knows that a man's role is to be a protector and a provider.
- He's not afraid to confront difficulties head-on.
- He's not a coward and doesn't hide behind excuses.
- He's not 'too' proud to learn what women are all about and make them feel safe and comfortable.
- He's independent, whether it is financially or from seeking women's opinions or advice.
- On the other hand, he's not afraid to ask for advice when the situation calls for it and listen to another's input.
- He leads the way and guides his woman.
- He's not afraid to show his sexual attraction to the woman he desires.
- He's not scared of being a man and of his intentions.
- He easily expresses his wants, needs and desires when the moment is right.
- He takes initiative and is responsible for his actions.
- He's not a yes-man. Instead, he behaves depending on what is just and right at that moment.
- He's not trying to please everyone all the time.
- He has a backbone and he shows it.
- He's a good negotiator.
- He's not easily swayed by insults, rejection or criticism. At least he doesn't show it. He has a thick skin.
- He's calm and doesn't feel the need to prove himself to anyone.
- He's passionate and not afraid to show it.

- He has a great sense of humor and is not afraid to make a slightly sexual joke or observation at the right moment.
- He's gentle to those weaker than him, but can stand up to aggression.
- He'll come to a woman's rescue in a precarious or dangerous situation.
- But at the same time, he's not going to jump through hoops for every woman's whim.
- He's in control but knows when to be vulnerable.
- He carries himself proudly and doesn't look for excuses.
- He recognizes the differences between men and women. He'll be rougher with the guys and gentler with the girls.
- With that comes sensitivity to women when necessary. This is the opposite from a macho guy who walks all over everyone.
- A man knows the difference between a situation where his strength is required vs. when he's called upon to be gentle, caring and compassionate.
- He's friendly to children and nice to animals.
- He projects a calm, self-assured image.

These last traits of sensitivity and compassion are key if you don't want to be a brainless macho and a jerk. A charming man is able to balance the different facets of his personality, and this includes also the more sensitive sides.

Now let's look at what defines a more feminine guy:

- He's trying to please anyone and everyone at the expense of his authenticity.
- He's a pushover.
- He'll try to prove himself to women as if he's not deserving of them.
- He'll put a woman on a pedestal.
- He'll first try to be friends with a woman, hiding his real intentions.
- He's not a leader, instead he's a follower, including with women.
- He doesn't take initiative and hides behind the excuse that he doesn't want to come off as too aggressive or not respectful to women. In reality, initiative and respect don't have to be exclusive.
- He's a complainer and often shifts responsibility to others.
- He leaves it up to the girl where to go on a date or what to do.
- He gives an aura of being a boring person.
- He's nervous around women, which often translates into awkwardness.
- His sensitiveness is an asset he doesn't put to use at the appropriate time.
- He's too afraid of women.
- He's wimpy.
- He gives in to his negative emotions and his insecurities.
- He walks with slouchy shoulders and doesn't maintain eye contact.

- He's constantly catering to the woman, which ends off throwing off balance in the interaction.
- He's afraid to take charge of a situation and takes the backseat.
- He lets the woman do the negotiating and the 'dirty work,' such as defending herself in a precarious situation.
- He doesn't know what he wants and instead lets the woman decide that for him.
- He's too easily swayed in his opinions.
- He's psychologically and emotionally weak.
- He has no drive or ambition to be someone in life.
- He always plays it safe and is afraid to take risks, to go for something head-on.

Now, what often gets ignored in many dating advice books and courses is that it's important to distinguish between a jerk and a good guy. They are not the same as a masculine and a feminine guy.

What I mean is that there are traits you DO NOT want to take from bad guys, and traits you DO NOT want to get rid of if you're a nice guy. Everyone always talks about nice guys finishing last. They only finish last when it comes down to attracting women. But they have many more characteristics that are important for long-term partnerships. The bad boys, on the other hand, have mastered the art of flirting and manipulating women, but if one day they want to be successful in a real relationship or get dumped by a smart girl, they're at a loss. That's when reality sets in and suddenly they realize that they need to work on themselves.

So, if you're one of those guys, do not feel bad about being a good person. Be proud about those traits and put them to work in the best possible way. Realize that you're only a few steps away from becoming attractive to women. And once you learn and practice to embody and put forward your more masculine traits, you'll be the full package for the girl. You'll be ahead of all the idiots and smart-asses out there who have no idea how to be a good partner in life and a good man.

Here are the good traits of a nice guy that you absolutely need to keep:

- Respecting women; being friendly and generous
- Being a gentleman
- Avoiding hurting, humiliating or disrespecting a woman
- Never forcing yourself physically on a woman or forcing her to do something sexual
- Having integrity and honesty
- Being sensitive to a woman and her needs
- Being compassionate and empathetic in general and toward women
- Not competing with a woman, whether verbally, in sports or in a career
- Not being selfish and narcissistic
- Taking into consideration what a woman likes and wants
- Being a good friend to a woman
- Being responsible and gentle
- Being nice and thoughtful
- Giving compliments

And here are some traits that you do not want to take on from jerks:

- Treating a woman poorly
- Disrespecting her and her schedule
- Putting her down or Criticizing her
- Being very self-centered or narcissistic
- Ignoring her when she's in pain or suffering
- Making fun of her or badmouthing her, whether it's to her face or to your friends
- Ignoring her desires and wants
- Taking advantage of her, whether financially, physically or emotionally
- Hurting her emotionally or in any other way
- Taking revenge on her if things don't work out
- Competing with her
- Always wanting to be right
- Always wanting to be first
- Being insensitive to her and her female differences
- Being rude and in general not be nice to her
- Dumping her like a rock
- Lying to her or misleading her
- Thinking that women should be submissive to men's whims and desires
- Manipulating her in any way
- Humiliating her publicly or in private
- Calling her a bitch or other names

- Dumping her in a bad way after a one-night stand, not explaining anything or not returning her phone calls
- Being vulgar and transgress her boundaries
- Pretending you're interested in something serious while all you want to do is get in her pants

These traits are nasty. It's the lowlifes of our modern world who embody those personality traits. If you want to become a man that is more evolved from the pack, do not behave in these nasty ways. Work on your shortcomings and always try to be your best self. The reason why women are suspicious of men is because there are many lowlifes out there. Don't be one. If you've picked up this book, chances are you're not. As any man who's working on improving himself, you're on the right path, no matter how fast or slow your journey is going. That's what life is all about. Never stop trying to do your best.

WHO YOU ARE

No one is perfect and no one is expecting you to be. As a matter of fact, I fully believe in the saying that perfection lies in the imperfection. Don't stress or pressure yourself about embodying the above traits and avoiding the bad ones. Instead, take it one step at a time and forgive yourself for any mistakes. The best way to learn is by trial and error, and with that come failures – no way around it. The key is to get out of your shell and start practicing.

An ideal man for a woman is a man who can balance the masculine and feminine sides of himself at the right time and place. He's not afraid of his feminine side. Instead, he embraces it. But he uses it in a constructive way when it's necessary to be sensitive to the girl he's with, when the situation calls for his compassion and understanding.

For the purpose of attraction and flirting, however, the great majority of your behavior needs to focus on the masculine traits and actions. You can squeeze in a few feminine traits depending on the moment. For example, if the girl is telling you something of her past that is hurtful, it is appropriate to show empathy and interest. You can say: "I'm sorry you had to go through that."

The key is to be courteous and friendly, but also confident and a leader. Review those lists and mark the traits you have and those you don't. Then brainstorm and practice those you'd like to acquire.

FLIRTING

DETACHMENT

To flirt successfully, you need to be DETACHED from the outcome. If it works, great. If it doesn't, you feel confident enough that the next one will be better. If you're too emotionally attached to the outcome, you will be planning and reciting stuff you've practiced. This will create stress and nervousness, not to mention it will appear artificial and rehearsed. It can quickly become a vicious cycle where one little mistake leads to you feeling more nervous and making more mistakes, which in the end turns to disaster.

Instead, you need to play it by ear. The way to get good at it is to practice, practice, practice. After a while, it will become your second nature. As they say, fake it 'til you make it. Start in small doses, then gradually work your way up to do and say more. To be detached, go about it as if it's your everyday way of being. Take a deep breath and accept whatever happens. Meanwhile, watch the reaction and the effects that your flirting creates on somebody. It's this feedback loop that will help you know what works and what doesn't. It will also help you be more in tune with women, what they like and what pushes them away, and what gets you noticed. All master womanizers have perfected that skill through practice and experience. And experience is made up of experimentation, of making mistakes and adjusting your course with the feedback loop.

TALKING

When talking to women, it's best to slow down your pace. A lower, deeper voice is usually more attractive than a high-pitched one.

Be aware of how you talk. Slow it down, don't rattle of a bunch of things and don't ramble. Say something, then stop and listen. Men are notoriously bad listeners. Well, here's your chance. Ask a question and listen. Then ask a follow-up question and listen again. Don't bring the subject back to yourself. Don't whine her ears off by constantly talking about you and your stories. This can become quickly uninteresting and she'll move on quite fast.

EXTERNAL FOCUS

To help yourself along, you can slow down your speech by pointing to something external, so that the focus shifts away from you for a moment. This will give you an extra second or two to pull yourself back together.

For example, you're at a party and you've just approached a girl. Instead of immediately asking her what's your name or where are you from, point to the bar tender and say: "Boy, is he busy tonight. He'll be earning lots of tips." Then pause for a second. See how she reacts. If she's receptive to your observation, you can continue. If she's rolling her eyes, turning her head away or not reacting whatsoever to you, ignore what just happened and go your way. No need to feel frustrated or hurt.

Or, let's say you're meeting her for the first time in a bistro after connecting with her online. You're arriving at the table where she's sitting. All of a sudden, you feel like a nervous wreck and are at a loss of words. Instead of artificially trying to find a subject of conversation, sit down and adjust the table. Then look at her and say: "This was quite a wiggly table, so I adjusted it, there you go." Then smile at her and say: "Hi, nice to meet you."

You're in a group setting, for example at a birthday party, and you're all sitting at a table; the girl across from you looks cute and you'd like to strike up a conversation with her. Instead of seriously asking her for her name, make a funny comment: "How's that steak? Looks like they just killed the cow." Or: "I should have gotten that dish, it looks so good on your plate."

Once you said it, the key is not to be all 'sticky,' meaning not hanging all over the girl. This needs to be done in a casual way and once you've made your comment, you're refocusing back on you or the general environment and not just monopolizing the girl. If you don't remove yourself after these types of comments, then you will appear desperate and awkwardly manipulative. So, just make your comment and continue as if nothing happened. Your approach needs to be gentle and paced, not rushed and sleazy.

It's that simple. Any time you're unsure about how to strike up a conversation, just use an external focus as a starter. From there, you can move into more detail about her.

It needs to be all cute and innocent, but with a very subtle sexual undertone. To achieve that undertone, add to the mix eye contact and facial expression. A mischievous or playful smile can go a long way. Look directly at the girl. This will be the best way to make a great first impression.

SILENCE IS GOLDEN

When there's a silence in the conversation, it may be tempting to try and fill in the blanks by saying just whatever comes to mind. That's a mistake. Don't fall into that trap.

Silence is an interesting moment to just let yourself and your girl be. When you're relaxed about a moment of silence, it shows confidence and it also gives you a bit of a mysterious air. Be natural and don't try to force a conversation when there's a natural break.

Instead, take advantage of that moment to look deeply in the eyes of the woman you're with and smile to her. Or you can take a deep breath in a relaxed sort-of-way and just show a moment of physical appreciation of the beautiful surroundings, nature or the wonderful moment you're both having. Remember, silence is golden, so don't ruin it.

LET'S TALK ABOUT...

What do you talk about with the girl and sound interesting and not awkward?

Talking about the weather won't cut it unless there is something unusual going on. Forget sports as it's a guy thing and you can't expect a woman you just met to be on the same page as you. Don't start with complimenting her physical appearance either as this comes off as too eager and women don't like being viewed as objects of a man's admiration.

Well, it's not as difficult as it sounds. Come off natural and don't overdo the 'macho' thing. This means avoiding showing off, arrogance, patronizing and other bad behavior. If you're a naturally goodhearted person, this should be easy. But if you're one of those alpha males who thinks that's what you need to show, you'd be way off. Being an alpha male doesn't mean you can act obnoxious, pretentious or focused solely on you.

So, the first thing is to make the conversation not about you, but rather about something you have in common with the girl.

In general, a successful encounter with a woman is made up of three conversation steps that I call *CEA*:

1) *Comfort*
2) *Emotion*
3) *Action*

There are different ways to accomplish these, so it gives you quite a bit of flexibility.

1. COMFORT

When you first enter the room and approach the girl or sit down at a table, start by building comfort. This sounds obvious but many guys don't know how to do that. They stumble over words and seem goofy or awkward.

Yet, it's a simple technique that instantly puts the other person at ease and breaks the ice. I've already touched upon this a bit earlier, but here are a few more ways to create comfort from the start.

The easiest way to make someone comfortable is by showing empathy, compassion, tolerance or a nonjudgmental attitude about something. This quickly not only shows a positive side of yours and a more sensitive side, but also puts the other person at ease about the fact that you don't expect perfection and that you're human.

For example, you can point out that you saw this old lady crossing the street and no one cared to help her, but you did. I am not urging you to lie, ok! Just point out something that shows you're a compassionate person.

Another example, this is one of the few times you can bring the conversation to you and point out that you're all in sweat as you were rushing through traffic to get here and meet with her. Put on a mischievous smile and pretend you're wiping off your forehead. Or, if you are indeed sweaty, wipe off your forehead and make a joke about yourself that is slightly degrading, such as: "I hope you don't mind my sweat," or, "Don't worry, I took a shower this morning." It's paramount to do this with a smile and a sparkle in your eyes so that this level of comfort is created with humor and lightness. If you're saying this too seriously, you may come off as weird. It needs to have an energy of charm. It will then show that you're comfortable with yourself, AND with the girl!

In general, any blunder or awkwardness can be quickly and completely erased with humor and a smile. Make this a habit of yours and you'll get through almost any situation.

If you're at a party, you can do the sweat gesture by saying that you had to fight the crowds to get just to her and that you apologize if you're all exhausted.

Another example is apologizing about the clothes you're wearing as you came straight out of work. Meanwhile, make sure you're actually wearing a nice and elegant suit that day. Again, don't forget that mischievous smile.

Try to build comfort and humor out of reality. Maybe you could barely understand the valet parking attendant, but the fact that he was nice and wearing white gloves meant that you could completely trust him with your Mercedes or old minivan. This shows compassion and manages to be a bit humorous simultaneously.

I hope by now you get what building comfort means. By insinuating that you're not looking for perfection, you both break the ice and make her feel more at ease. This is important, as most guys put too much pressure on themselves by trying to be perfect and that's when things go wrong. A confident man could care less about those situations and is not afraid to show his human side.

2. EMOTION

After you've put her and yourself at ease and done some small talk, it's a good idea to sprinkle here and there something that shows your vulnerability and sensitivity as a person. It's a similar philosophy as creating comfort, but here you're presenting a deeper and more serious side of yourself and are showing that you are comfortable with your past or with something that happened to you.

This is where you can go into a recent breakup, or the fact that you've become more emotional over the years and now cry when you watch a sad movie, or that you can't stand it when you hear about discrimination or sexism in the media.

If you're a little bit older, you can say that experience is made up of all the mistakes one makes in one's life, and so you're a very experienced man. Make sure it doesn't come off as too heavy. And leave it at that. This will show a bit of wisdom and introspection on your part. As a result of showing a bit of this vulnerability, you will endear yourself in the eyes of the woman you're with.

Another example is talking about how you love animals. Perhaps your dog/cat was sick, and this saddened you greatly. Basically, show a bit of heart. Don't just be all in your head and mental. The key is to show you're an emotional human being. This is also what will allow you to connect with the person and help you open up various topics, such as asking her if she likes animals, etc.

Beware though about digging too deep into the past or disclosing too personal of information about abuse, neglect, a bad divorce, etc. This can quickly scare someone off as you not being completely healed from your past or stuck with some issues of anger or depression. It's ok to mention it when you get to know the person later, but not this soon. Even if she asks you some of those questions, answer honestly, but move on to another topic. Asking a question and listening is the best way to switch topics.

A good transition from something sad or heavy is to plainly say: "let's talk about fun and happy things, such as why you moved into town? I am sure you have an interesting story or two to tell."

The indirect result from the comfort and emotion stages is that it helps to build a strong connection with the woman of your desire. And this is your goal. After all, you're talking with her to see if this can go any further or at the very least to get a good feel for her personality.

3. ACTION

Action is what happens in the second part of the flirting or conversation. Once you've opened up about a few personal things and have her open up as well, you need to take some leadership and show you're a man of action.

This can be done in small or large ways. Small action items include calling the waiter, asking the waiter to refill her glass, asking for the dessert menu, asking if she'd like another drink, etc. Little things like that can be done throughout the date.

But when you're getting toward the end, your head needs to be thinking about what to do next. This can include everything such as checking how she parked and if she has enough time left in the parking meter, or looking at your watch and saying that you know of another bar that doesn't close until a later time, so maybe you can move your evening there.

Anything that relates to taking an action, even if it's moving across the room, will do. What you're doing here is showing that you know how to lead, that you're not hanging on every word of hers, that you're a man who knows what he wants and how to behave around women. Beware not to overdo it or be too abrupt, as it can come off as too artificial or programmed.

It needs to be a natural progression as you spend time with her.

Follow these three steps of comfort, emotion and action, and you'll have a smoothly flowing time with the girl you're with. It will also show that you're not just hanging there and drooling all over her.

CONVERSATION TACTICS

When conversing with a woman, it's important to maintain a certain balance, or you will have an immediate power shift to either your way or her way, and that's never productive. If you want to build that sexual tension between the two of you, it's paramount not to talk all the time, nor to let her talk all the time.

I call the ideal conversation between a man and a woman a 'ping-pong' game: you throw something, then she throws something, then you respond, then she responds, and so forth. This is what makes it interesting, balanced and mature.

If you talk too much, you'll appear too eager, self-centered or crazy. If you let her ask all the questions and lead the conversation, she'll quickly find you boring and lacking leadership skills, not to mention having a low self-esteem.

So, while you can gently lead the conversation, it needs to constantly fluctuate from you to her and back to you and back to her, just like in a ping-pong game. It needs to be light and natural, not heavy and constricted. It takes practice to achieve this. Some people, such as those who are good at sales, have a natural inkling toward a smooth conversation. Others will need to learn and practice.

Also, avoid interview-like settings or a conversation where too much Q&A takes place. This will certainly disrupt the flow and will quickly turn off the other person.

Another thing to avoid is asking questions that are too personal or too sensitive. It's usually too soon to dig deep into another person's secrets or sensitive areas. So, while your conversation may have touched upon a few of those elements, be careful not to get stuck in them. Instead, refocus the subject on something fun and wistful.

Some men make the mistake of correcting a woman. It could be her use of the language, an accent or adding a 'please' or a 'thank you' at the end of the sentence. This is a big no-no. Unless she asked you to do that, making any kind of correction will make YOU come off as rude or aggressive. It will also give you a patronizing air and that's not a good way to make a first impression.

MAKING STATEMENTS

One of the ways to avoid falling into the interview-style conversation is instead of asking too many questions, saying the same thing in the form of a statement.

For example, instead of asking your girl: "Where did you go to school?" you could make a statement such as: "You must have gone to a Southern school if you like that style of cuisine."

Making statements can be done with just about any subject and once you've done it a couple of times, it will be very easy to apply it when flirting with a girl.

In addition, statements also give you the opportunity to give a compliment without appearing too eager or too artificial. You could say: "You must be very organized to work, raise kids, take care of your pets and have your hobbies all at the same time without having any help."

She will most likely elaborate on your statement or smile and say something about you. And that's good as it will allow you to pursue the conversation, and flirting, in a subtle and interesting way. Your ping-pong game will continue as it should.

Just beware of making cheesy statements or saying things that could come off slightly insulting. Sarcasm is best reserved for external observations and not so much to make a statement about the woman you're with.

For example, if you're talking about business and leadership, and you make the statement, "You're not a leader," this can quickly offend her. Even if it's true, most people don't want to hear this and they probably know that about themselves anyways. Maybe you're looking for a girl that's not so much of a leader and that's fine. But you don't want to say this to her face as maybe she's striving to be a leader or is frustrated that she's not a leader in her field.

If you're running out of ideas, you can always make a statement about something around you: the restaurant, bar, party, venue, etc. That way you don't take any risks. This loses the purpose of getting closer to her by showing her you're observant about who she is, but it's just another way to start the conversation. And when you're more comfortable about her and feel you can make a correct statement with confidence, then go for it.

Here are some examples:

- It must take a lot of courage to do what you did.
- It must have been difficult to go through that turbulent time.
- I'm impressed with women who make it a point to keep up with technology.
- No wonder you meditate a lot. Having such a stressful job needs an outlet.
- You must use both the left and right halves of your brain if you're able to do math and be an artist at the same time.
- You're quite an independent woman and that's very attractive to me, even though some men get intimidated by it.
- You must have a heart of gold if you're finding time to volunteer in the shelter in addition to everything else you have going on.
- You have quite a sense of humor. Did you learn it when you were in college or is it part of your family genes?

CREATING AND USING HOOKS

Hooks are a fantastic way to keep the conversation flowing. You can create a hook by asking open-ended questions or making statements. The point that you make at the end of your sentence (or even within the sentence) will be a hook for the girl to continue on and keep conversing. When she says something that leads to an interesting hook, use this to move the conversation in that direction.

Using hooks will make a conversation interesting and exciting. It can even create a certain chemistry and connection as you'll be finding things in common to talk about.

Here's how this could flow:

She: I work downtown, so sometimes I get stuck in traffic on my way there. (The hook here could be traffic.)

You: Ah, traffic can be really bad going that way. How long does it take you? (You've just created a hook about the time it takes her.)

She: Sometimes I'm stuck on the freeway for 50 minutes to an hour. I've missed several meetings in the mornings because of that. (New hook: meetings/work.)

You: (Using humor and smiling) You should ask your boss to accommodate you and start the meetings later. He wouldn't want to miss your input, wouldn't he? (Indirect compliment)

She: Ha, thanks for thinking I'm so important, but I'm just there to take notes and make a report of the meeting.

You: But you are important, your boss just doesn't know it yet. Wait till he's the one who has to speak and write at the same time. (Saying it with a smile) By the way, you women are just masters at multitasking. I wish I could do as many things at the same time as you do. How do you do that? (New hook women/multitasking.)

She: Well, I guess we're just wired that way. That's why we should get paid more (She laughs.)

You: Yes, you're right. You totally deserve higher pay! And not just that, you women are superior in so many ways (A little ego stroking – women have egos too, by the way; and a new hook for her: superior.)

She: Oh, yes, we're superior in cooking, and many other things. (She says with a smile.)

You: There you go. I can barely make a hard-boiled egg. By the way, what's the best kind of meal a man ever made for you? (That's more flirtatious and intriguing and creates a new hook.)

And so on and so forth! See how it flows, how you make it light and fluffy? You make her feel great, you're giving her a bit of importance, you're using humor and you're moving the conversation along, instead of getting stuck on the same subject. That's also a way to change the subject if you or she are uncomfortable with something.

GIVING COMPLIMENTS

It's important to give compliments to a woman, but it needs to happen in a natural and subtle way. If you're overdoing it or are too direct about it, it will quickly turn her off. That's why compliments are best worked into the conversation in an indirect way.

Making statements such as, "You are a beautiful woman; you must have tons of guys chasing after you," is not just cheesy and ordinary, but you will also make her feel instantly uncomfortable. It will be as if you're putting her on the spot, or worse, on the pedestal.

No woman wants to feel objectified or viewed as a sex symbol (even if that's the kind of vibe she gives off to you). Making comments on her physical appearance, whether it's her body, face or dress, is a no-no.

Also, if you comment on her physical appearance, you can turn her off by appearing inexperienced and desperate. Experienced players and successful men don't do that. They feel comfortable around beautiful women and so do not feel compelled to comment on their looks. If you're making statements of a woman's beauty, it will send her the message that you're not used to dating or courting attractive women. And this will diminish your value instantly in her eyes. Never compliment a woman on her looks, unless you've already had a few dates with her and she's, for example, dressed for a special occasion, in which instance it would be appropriate to make a positive comment about it. But just saying, "you're so beautiful," or, "you have beautiful eyes," or anything else of the sort will not make you stand out as she's probably heard it before. She wants to know that you're looking to get to know the real her, not the external shell. And that comes with conversation and action.

So, what kind of compliments can you give then? Abstaining from physical aspects is key. But you can easily give her compliments about her personality or character. This will score you many points as it will showcase that you're attentive, that you're smart and observant and that you care.

You can make statements as in the examples above where you work in compliments indirectly.

Another way is to make humorous statements and smile, without expecting any kind of response from her.

And finally, you can make a compliment about her to someone else in her presence. That's a great way to indirectly say something positive, but not come off as too eager or artificial. Beware not to come off patronizing though, as this can quickly happen. The compliment needs to be gentle and somewhat neutral.

More examples:

- I think we're getting some extra fast service here. Must be because of your presence. Otherwise it seems like I always get the slowest waiter in the room.
- Look, the sun came out. The weatherman must like you. Do you always have this effect on people? (This will make her smile and maybe even blush.)

- I've never seem someone flipping her hair like you. You've got quite a way with it. (Even though it's physical appearance you're talking about, it's a very specific aspect you're talking about and it relates more to her actions than her hair, so it makes your compliment unique.)

- You must be very close to your family. That's something so precious few people realize when they have it, until they lose it.

- Speaking to the waiter: "Please bring us the appetizers quickly as we must feed this young lady. She just accomplished a huge feat by doing the marathon walk."

- Speaking to your friends and in front of your girl: "Anna is quite the world traveler, she's been to over 40 countries. That's even more than me!"

- Speaking to your family (when she's there): "Megan speaks 5 languages. I can barely write in one."

TEASING

Teasing is a great way to gently push someone's boundaries and challenge them a bit. But it's not as easy as it sounds as you could insult a girl if you tease her in the wrong way. When done right, teasing will create a flirtatious response back and will augment sparks between the two individuals.

For example, if the girl tells you that she's always losing her car keys and that's why she's late, you don't want to say something like "oh, so you're a disorganized klutz." Even if you say this with a smile, it will be in insult as it's a direct description and judgment of what she told you. Instead, you can say something funny such as "As long as you don't lose your beautiful accent (or sense of humor), I'll be happy to wait."

When mastered in the right way, teasing is a very effective flirting technique. You just need to make sure it always stays positive and comes from a place of kindness, not meanness.

You can also use teasing as a polite way of pointing something negative out or to laugh off an issue. If the girl says she can't find any of her friends at the party, reply that maybe she's on purpose avoiding them just so she can meet you. You'll happily let her look for them if she comes back to you for a drink.

Or, maybe she had a disagreement with a neighbor and is rather frazzled on the date. You can tease her by saying that it's not her fault if she has such a strong effect on people. Another example could be she is surprised that she drank that cocktail so fast. You joke back that your presence must be making her nervous or that you'll have to find someone else to drop you off at the train station.

SEXUAL INNUENDO

Flirting can contain some sexual references. Notice that I say CAN, not HAS TO. A lot depends on the situation, the person you're with and your goal. Often, people overdo on the sexual innuendo and come off as vulgar or too direct. It's an area where finesse of language is critical. You'll show you have some sophistication and experience in that department if you use sexual innuendo sparsely.

The best way to achieve this is to sprinkle sexy words here and there but keep your composure and posture serious or nonchalant. What I mean is that don't make it a point to say something sexual or sensual. Instead, weave it into a phrase.

For example: use the words delicious, sumptuous, splendid, fantastic, sensuous, etc. to describe seemingly ordinary things, such as a delicious day, a sumptuous place, a sensuous dish or a splendid outfit. Say it casually and don't show in your body or facial language that you meant to sound a little sexual when you said it. It needs to come off as a natural way of speaking for you.

In general, it is sexy when a man uses vocabulary that not everyone does. So, if you can showcase a richer use of words or slightly mismatched combinations of words that sound sexier or show that you're very observant, you'll score points. It will also show off your way of interpreting situations or noticing things, so make it positive and don't worry if you exaggerate a bit with your 'splendid' description. It will get you noticed.

Many guys make the mistake of using sexual talk left and right in the conversation and being overly direct. This is a sign that you're not very experienced and that you must have picked up on this type of lingo somewhere in a course or from friends. Try to avoid these kinds of expressions as you'll annoy the girl. The whole point of flirting and using sexual innuendo is subtlety. If it's overly obvious, it will lose its mystery and appeal. So, refrain from using sweety, honey, gorgeous and other descriptors that risk coming off as sleazy, especially at the beginning. When you know the person better, you can slowly weave in some of the more obvious phrases, but use it more jokingly and again, sparingly.

EXAGGERATION

Another way to smooth out a conversation or show that you can laugh at stuff that you disagree on is to agree and exaggerate.

Perhaps she mentions that all men are jerks and she has yet to find one that will not flake on her. Instead of going on the defensive and trying to explain or prove that you're not one of them, make the whole thing lighter by saying: "No, really? And have you noticed, they're also all afraid of commitment and to top it off, are cheapskates." This will most likely make her laugh and show her that you're not easily bruised. Instead, you're confident to joke about your own sex and can stand a small critique.

When something is said that can supposedly be taken personally or offensively, turn it into something lighter by amplifying the statement to the point of absurdity. This will relax the atmosphere between the two of you and will put you in a playful mood, which is key to successful flirting.

ROLE PLAYING

Speaking of playfulness, once in a while you can use role playing as a way to relax the atmosphere. As with all the tricks, avoid using it the second you meet the person or being too obvious in what you'd like to achieve.

To be successful at role playing, it needs to be done in a playful way and you need to keep it short. Don't go overboard with it and don't force the girl to participate if you see that she's not too keen about it.

Here's an example:

She: So, what do you do for a living?

You: How 'bout I give you three guesses before I disclose it? (Here, you can make it fun and elaborate on each guess.)

She: You're in finance.

You: And what makes you think that? (You're giving her a chance to explain why she thinks that.)

She: You're well dressed and you seem good with numbers.

You: Thanks for the compliment. Next?

She: Hmmmm, you're a business coach?

You: Closer. So how do I fit into that category?

She: Well, you're personable and seem to go into the depth of things.

You: Good point, warmer. Third and final guess?

She: You're in sales. And that's because you know how to talk well and how to get people intrigued into what you're saying.

You: Well, thanks again. These are quite some qualities. You guessed it right, I do pharmaceutical sales. But enough about me, what about you? Or do I need to guess three times as well?

See how this becomes a fun game where you're able to find out more about each other while at the same time being playful and even possibly establishing a bond? Now, this example talks about you, but in general, I would suggest you focus on the girl. So instead of having her guess, see if you can guess stuff about her. This would score you more points as it would show your interest in her, instead of obligating her to focus on you. I gave you this example to show you how to role play, but try to focus more on her and avoid bringing the topic back to you too early in the game or too often.

Let's say she guesses your star sign. You can then say that you'll guess three times before she'll need to tell you hers. Make it playful:

You: OK, so now's my turn. I'm allowed three guesses, right? After that I owe you a drink if I haven't guessed. And if I did guess, then you owe me a drink, deal?

She: Deal.

You: My first guess is Leo.

She: Ha, why do you think that?

You: Because you have the posture and hair of a lioness. (You introduce a sexy compliment.) Plus, you're beaming of warmth and I believe Leos are known for that.

She: OK, guess No. 2?
You: Hmmm, what else… Maybe Aries?

She: Aries?

You: Yeah, you seem to know what you want and ready to get it too. Aries are bold and you don't strike me as being too shy.

She: Interesting. Last one?

You: Hard to guess. How 'bout Sagittarius?

She: Ohhh, so what do I have of a Sag?
You: I have no clue, but this just came to me. (You're saying this with a smile.) So, time for the verdict!

She: You were totally off. I'm a Pisces. But thanks for the compliments! Hmmm, what kind of drink shall I order?

This is how easy it can be to play with words, flirt and make it fun. So use these techniques when appropriate and be original. You'll create chemistry and a bond in no time.

Us Against Them

Another tactic is to set something up where you're forming a team and competing against someone else (without telling them). This is an effective way of creating a bond between the two of you and also makes things fun and unique.

For example: if you're attending a casino night, team up to play together at blackjack or some other game and secretly try to amass the most money vs. the others. Most people really like doing these activities and it can make your night special.

Or, you can set up an "us against them" situation where you try to order a better and more impressive dish than the couple at another table. Let's say you're at a sushi place and you see that the waiter just brought a beautiful sushi selection on a Japanese wooden bridge. And you see on the menu that the next (and bigger) dish is a sushi platter on a wooden boat. You order it and joke how you're going to have an even nicer dinner! Make it fun and even somewhat sensuous by enjoying some top-class sushi. You can do a similar thing with cocktails or appetizers – it doesn't always need to be expensive.

If you're at a bar, you can joke about how you'll get the attention of the bartender ahead of the others. And every time you need a drink, you joke around and see if you can be the first ones to have the bartender serve you.

Other situations include finding the shortest line in the supermarket, at the airport gate or winning a sports game if you're playing a sport.

Your options are limitless. Just make sure not to make it too serious and instead have fun with it.

TOUCH

Touch can be used effectively during flirting, but it's important to know how and when. Women have strong physical boundaries and it's paramount for men not to intrude on those or she'll run away faster than you can blink.

The only touching I recommend is if you're really feeling the conversation is flowing well and you're establishing a good connection. In this situation, you can briefly touch her arm, shoulder or on the back just above the waist line while moving to another spot or making an interesting suggestion in the conversation. Make sure you do this toward the end of your interaction. Ideally, you would do this on the second date. However, it's ok to do it the first time around if you really feel a strong connection.

Please avoid touching first thing when you meet a girl, touching multiple times or being too rough in your touch. It needs to be very gentle – barely perceptible. You can also use physical touch or action in situations such as helping her with her jacket, moving her purse closer to her so that there's no risk of pick pockets, moving her chair out for her to sit, opening the door for her, etc. It doesn't always need to be a direct touch on her physical body, though obviously this one creates a higher level of intimacy.

CHEMISTRY

While we're naturally compatible with some people and not with others, a lot of the chemistry can be created on the spot. Sure, destined couples often feel an uncontrollable draw to each other, no matter their looks or even their conversation. We all want this type of connection. But experienced men know that it's quite rare and so they've become masters at creating the feeling of chemistry with the woman they desire.

Obviously, they won't pursue just any woman, so there are some elements of attraction already there. But you need to remember that women are mostly attracted to men who are charming, eloquent, confident, classy and masculine yet sensitive at the same time. And these aspects are in your control. Even if you feel that you're falling short in one area or another, you can learn those skills and with practice, you will exude an energy that will become irresistible to many women.

So, how do you create chemistry?

A lot of it has already been discussed above. It's a combination of many components and characteristics that women find attractive in men. But even when you feel that she's not totally open to you, you can work with the energy of charm, eye contact and humor to make a woman more comfortable and more open to your advances.

When you create emotional links (discussed earlier) with the girl, you will make her feel more relaxed and you'll create a certain bond between you. Also, simple things like discussing common interests, throwing in a potential plan to go somewhere and playing on her words or using humor will all reinforce your relationship with her.

You can be an ugly, short guy, but when you've mastered your behavior around women, you'll be able to get the girls that previously wouldn't even look at you. Now, while I say this, if you want to put all your luck on your side, I suggest you try to find girls that are around the same level as you: intellectually, look-wise, age-wise, etc. And to my point, have you noticed how couples often look alike, almost like a brother and sister? I don't think it's coincidence. It's because they're naturally and physically compatible. Don't obsess with some gorgeous 6-foot tall girl when you realize she's out of your league. If you want to build up confidence after many failures, I recommend you start 'small' and approach girls that would be not so hard to catch. Then, with practice, you'll reach success with an ever-increasing venue of impressive women.

Building trust, rapport and connection are very important factors in the game of flirting and seduction. This often comes down to how you make the woman feel and not so much about how you feel. To be able to do this, you need to be more aware and in control of your emotions, and instead focus more of your attention on her.

At some point in your conversation (but not too early on), you can look profoundly into her eyes. Just hold eye contact a bit longer than usual, but don't overdo it. Try to maintain a deep gaze for about 3-5 seconds and don't say anything. This can make her slightly shy or uncomfortable and she may turn her head away a few times, but try to maintain your gaze. It needs to be friendly and 'pure,' not too flirtatious. It's rather a warm and serious look. A look that goes from your soul to hers. This will most likely melt her and you'll build yet another emotional link with her.

Also, just showing respect toward the woman and making her feel central is essential during the whole conversation. Some men make the mistake of doing all the flirting techniques with a girl they met at a party and then, trying to maximize their chances, move on to another girl and applying the same techniques there as well. When you do this, you will alienate the first girl as she'll notice you doing this.

There was a guy who went to a St. Patrick's party wearing a green tie. I observed him as he made his rounds of the room and went from one girl to the next making the same joke about how he had to go into his closet of 'horrors' to pull out some green tie to come to this event. What do you think happened? He sounded ridiculous, as everyone was in close quarters and several girls overheard him saying this repeatedly. I don't think he got many phone numbers that night. His conversation was shallow and it didn't make any girl feel special.

So, if you want to increase your chances, I suggest you focus on one girl a night and instead of having a superficial conversation with her, see if you can connect on a deeper level. You can even pull her aside so that the two of you can talk away from the noise. This will concentrate your attention on her and your chances of piquing her interest and securing her phone number will be much greater.

Most men who are experienced at flirting understand women very well. They know what women are looking for, how they will react, what their dating lives tend to be and the challenges of being a woman. When you take the time to study up on female desires and behaviors, you'll be able to better calibrate your behaviors around women. You will also exemplify that you have experience, and this too will attract a higher class of women.

A popular misconception is that an alpha male is all about himself and action, whereas the woman is merely a follower. Truly, though, a sophisticated male has studied women and is sensitive to their needs and desires at the right moment. Which leads us to the next chapter.

BALANCING ACT

Lately, a lot has been written about how to be an alpha male and how that's the only type of man that women fall for. I disagree. Women love nice men and men who treat them with respect, consideration and romance. What sets alpha males apart is their natural leadership ability, and this is primarily what women like. But alpha males also have a lot of shortcomings, one of which is their typical failure at long-term relationships.

Also, when you look in the kingdom of animals, there'll be only one alpha male per pack, so it's rare to be an alpha man. It's the same with humans. Not everyone is alpha. And that's alright! As a matter of fact, society's focus on celebrating the 'alpha male' has detracted people from real values. Not only is this not the real picture, but it's made many other, totally eligible, men feel insecure about who they are. If you're not an alpha male, that doesn't mean you can't be with a woman. It is fundamental to remember to balance out male and female energies within you, so that you can channel both when appropriate.

I've covered a lot of it early in this book, but below are the three main characteristics that women look for in men. I call them the LPP: Leader, Protector and Provider. Whether you're flirting for something casual or for something more serious, exhibiting the three traits will enhance your value in the eyes of the girl.

1) Leader

The primary aspect of an alpha man is leadership. This may not be so easy for you to display if you're not a natural leader, so I'll share with you some tricks on how to showcase leadership skills without feeling inauthentic.

First, some guys try to perform alpha male behaviors and fail terribly because it comes off as staged. A woman will immediately lose respect if she senses the guy is trying to falsely display macho behavior. So, refrain from doing and overdoing in this area.

The best way to be a leader is to master some basic dating skills. This includes setting dates and choosing places to go to, walking into the restaurant first and asking for a table, walking the girl to a quieter corner to talk to her, opening the door for her, refilling her glass or ordering her a drink. These small, practical gestures are most of what showing leadership is all about.

Another way of showing that you're a leader is to be able to stand up for yourself or to negotiate for something, such as exchanging a dish or getting a lower price for a car. When you do that, you show that you have a backbone and that you're not a wuss. That's very sexy for a woman. Remember to do this politely, though. Otherwise you'll quickly turn into a jerk. Remember, women need men for stuff that they can't do easily.

Alpha males take it a step further and that's an area where it can backfire. They may want to control everything about the date and what the woman does or wants. They may show arrogance or show that they don't care. They may flake on calling her. They may just talk about themselves during the dinner and not show any interest in her. See the point? These are jerks. Sure, they may be attractive – for a little while. But this is not what women really are looking for and most will not pursue anything with a man that shows the bad side of being alpha.

Instead of obsessing about being alpha, pick out 3 to 5 strong character traits of yours that you can showcase and use those when appropriate. It will open many doors for you (no pun intended).

2) Protector

Another important trait women are looking for is a man who can protect them. This doesn't need to be shown in a literal sense unless the situation calls for it, such as if someone is being obnoxious to the girl.

What you want to do is show that you're there for her if something happens. This can even be a small gesture, such as offering yourself as a contact if she's ever in trouble. That's another way of also sharing your phone number if you haven't done so yet.

Being a protector can include little things such as proposing to walk her to her car, wait for her somewhere and go together to a place or event, defend her from an indirect insult from others at a party, or side with her if she's telling you about an issue she's facing.

Protection is important to many women, as it's something most cannot do themselves. Even buying her pepper spray or having her follow your car safely wherever you're going shows that you care about her safety.

3) Provider

Obviously, everyone likes someone with money or a good job. Not everyone is in a situation like that. When you show a woman that you can take care of her financially, it's a big bonus. Just don't advertise it off the bat when you meet her. You don't want to appear as a show-off and that you're using this as a bait for her to like you. Instead, it needs to be communicated indirectly.

But what about guys who are not so financially secure? Well, that's when your personality needs to shine so that you can offset any worries the girl may have. Avoid discussing your struggles and instead show her a good time. This is also when being a nice guy will really play to your advantage. Women are constantly mistreated by jerks and if you happen to treat her nicely and have an interesting conversation with her, you may just be able to win her over.

Besides having a great personality, another way to get around the financial situation is to show that you have goals and projects. Women love men who know what they want. So, instead of getting stuck in a pity party about your situation, focus on what you're doing, what dream you're pursuing or what you'd like to achieve in 1, 3 or 10 years.

Finally, chivalry and generosity also show that you're a provider. Pay for the dates as much as you can. Don't accept that she pays in the beginning. If you're tight with money, then choose activities that are less expensive and sprinkle something more expensive here and there for refreshment. Only after several dates may you accept that she leaves a tip or shares something with you – but not at every date.

In today's day and age, women look for financial security. I am not talking about gold diggers. These are women with breasts hanging out, super short skirts and flashy behavior. Those girls will push you into spending huge amounts of money on them and that's all they have going for them. The women I am referring to are normal girls. This includes those who work, study, single moms, average-looking ones and even pretty ones who are not dressed like 'hookers.' Be respectful of a woman who's trying to be independent and make a living. It is still harder for women to have the same advancement options at work or to get the same payTreat them as much as you can. It's not about the money. It's about being a gentleman and showing that you're a provider at all costs.

ENERGY

To conclude this book, let's talk about energy. Everything is energy: all that you do, say and don't say. Be aware of this. This is why 60% of communication happens in a non-verbal form. Train yourself to be the best man that you can be. Always try to improve on yourself. It's the internal light that shines that ends up attracting women. Sure, your looks may get you by for a while, but you'll only attract the right woman with the light you shine.

That light is made up of everything that you are, everything that she sees and also what she perceives subconsciously. Energy is also about her, the environment you're in and your state of mind. Cultivate a positive attitude. View life as an optimist. Try to see the glass as half full. Show that you care. This energy will travel between you and her and create sparks. Observe women and observe men. Decide what you like and what you don't like in both. And believe when the time is right, things will work out in your favor, no matter what mistakes you make. Destiny is always on your side. Enjoy the journey!

SPREAD THE WORD

I hope you liked the book and found the advice and tips helpful. If you can please take just a few minutes and **review my book on Amazon** - it will help spreading the word and providing much-needed info to other men.

Thanks in advance and till soon!

Stella

Made in the USA
Columbia, SC
30 April 2018